ATHENIANS GO TO WORK

ATHENIANS GO TO WORK

by

YANNIS GOUMAS

THE SCEPTRE PRESS
Knotting • Bedfordshire

First published in 1978
by The Sceptre Press
Knotting Bedfordshire MK44 1AF England
Printed in Greece by
The Athens Publishing Center

ISBN 0 7068 0408 2

ACKNOWLEDGEMENTS

Some of these poems have appeared, or are due
to appear, in the following magazines: *Iron;
Tribune; Samphire; Diversion.*

CONTENTS

I wanted to write a poem   7
Dyspepsia   10
Case history   11
Exported on drawback   12
Defence budget   14
And now it's Mr Carter!   15
Armenian lament   17
Shipyard hand   18
Better things for better living
    through provocation   19
Road gang   20
Crew List, as a form of prayer   21
Street scene   23
On the dole   24
Athenians go to work   25
Homeward thoughts   27
Despite being a poet   29
Noblesse oblige   30
The stained-glass windows
    of Metz Cathedral   31
Corcovado   32
Copacabana   33
Hard times   34
Waiting for Taner Baybars   35
Coming of age   36
About my poetry   37

Publications   39
The author   41

I WANTED TO WRITE A POEM

I wanted to write a poem about the Fourth of July
      despite all it has cost us
            and it may have cost us very much.
I wanted to write about those pilgrim visions
long dimmed behind prescription glasses
as if no tongue had ever questioned yet
      who buys and who is bought
            who sells and who is sold.
I wanted to write this poem
because
      on the Fourth of July
            each year
my heart goes galloping on handkerchiefs
embroidered with forbearance.
Because
    too
      once upon a time
my love stretched taut from Coast to Coast
until America let go
      and forty-eight States curled
            like pubic hairs.
I wanted to write this poem
but the days passed
      that are easy to return from
            and there's no risk.

So I shall write a poem about a poem
written fifty years ago
      — August 12, to be exact —
whose author
unappeased by fame or prison
      sought like a child the eyes of justice
            to promise everything that matters.

Title: *Sacco and Vanzetti*:
victims of a nation
        that's made a highway
                        through the needle's eye:
two murdered deaths
        which caused a power cut
                        between heaven and earth.
Sacco and Vanzetti:
cognate names roughened by American twang:
grown too distant to divert
        from the cold tenter
                        of oblivion.

Sacco and Vanzetti:
reinstated after fifty years as ghosts
endangering All-American souls:
privileged now to choose any other death
that may have made them comrade to the earth —
                        any death!

Here's to you, Nicola and Bart . . .
hymn that haunts the Pontius Pilates of America
that sets them rushing
to the rivers
        to the lakes
                the waterfalls
                        and puddles
to wash innocent blood off their hands . . .

And the poet

who was married to that fervent prison dream of freedom
who was a page of sun always warm in the turning
who held in his translucent hands humanity's lost sight

the poet

whose protest jerked the world with four thousand volts
who splintered into stars when the chasm reached for him

his name: NAZIM HIKMET

August 2, 1977

DYSPEPSIA

Not that I love this country
a granule less than the next man,
but feeding Capitols and Kremlins to the poor
with the martial passion for peace,
and pointing at targets
with the social arthritis of index fingers,
will neither soften the flints of pain
nor dampen the mercury of instincts.

An empty belly goes with playing the bouzouki;
but does an empty belly go with playing Bach?

CASE HISTORY

Our temples are no longer ambitious
and they can lose antiquity in but a day.
This case history is one endless Halloween:
our sun sunned on American braid.

EXPORTED ON DRAWBACK

It's time
    it's really time
        to begin with an obituary.
Columns rise and come to nothing
as brittle as any moment's brief desire.
And the gods have departed
carrying with them
      on a silver dollar
            the mintage of sunlight.
The thing you're after
is a scene made up by the heart
and if you insist on being life-prone:
well
      now
        how do you like your life?
Well-done or rare?
Tut, tut!
All you have to say
    or need to know
        is neoned in for you.
Nouns
like
    "freedom"
        "justice"
            and "equality"
are grouped as homosexual.
You're better off
    asking for croutons
        served in soup.
The thing you're after
    merely displays the physiognomy
      of long-term decay.

So after centuries of suffering
from deprivation's idiom
it's time
        it's really time
                to turn intrepid scouts of talent.
Meanwhile
        pay no heed
                to that M.G.M. roar:
it is meant to drive you
to the scrimmage of appetite
                        everywhere.

DEFENCE BUDGET

Consider this:
Every male born is in fact a conscript;
and one can only surmise
that why the whole nation isn't unemployed
is the initial cost of freedom.

AND NOW IT'S MR CARTER!

Some statesmen think
that they can wipe the mess
generated by their predecessor
with tissue after tissue.
Theirs is a need for showy endings:
        healthy with haemorrhage,
        this is modern life.
No sooner sworn in
      than they practice levitation:
willing themselves six inches from God's ways.
(That's as far as *In God We Trust* goes.)
Beneath them
    the eavesdropped earth
      is a profile of buttocks;
and in that part overcome
by the deception of sunlight
millions go uphill for miles to meet them,
opening their mouths to let the promise enter,
giving their faces leave
    to fade
      from features.

We are on page 1978 in history's addendum,
and I am not aware of how the earth's
dark part fits into the scene.
People have either taken God seriously
or have become numinous with - *isms*.
Woe to those caught
    in a scissor
      of impossible light.
They get born,
and despair into lives.

They merely trespass
        on a virulence
                natural to the earth
and waste themselves for spindly limits.
The law moves among them
in nuances and imperatives.
It basks its claws outside
the well-trimmed light,
and their plead is a flower pressed sapless
in the pages of a book.

I can think of no sadness greater than
a soldier on a sunlit beach
and can imagine no kinder gesture than
to have Wall Street blown up to smithereens.
But I'm much too far out all my life,
                        n'est-ce pas?
Much further out than you thought.
Fellow-rankers all,
                we have a heart for a fool.
The right heart chosen for the wrong reason.
And the ingenuity of concealing it
stops us thinking of other things.

And now it's Mr Carter's pianoforte smile
that distracts the desperation.

ARMENIAN LAMENT

If bygones be bygones,
then others' bygones
            insulate
                    the fields of slaughter.
All life these fields have made a claim on therapy;
but other censuses have camouflaged our losses.
It isn't wheat
        it isn't corn
                    the sepia that you see:
it is our nation's suffering colour.
God knows
I'm trying to do without ghosts
— and God withdrew when his sons implored,
their claw marks raking along his side —
but when the wind stops
there's altogether too much room around everything
and I am shocked to find nothing that's a bygone.

SHIPYARD HAND

18

grey-faced as the steel plate
you deftly coax into position
with only two blue eyes
to variegate the din
you glance at my approach
and muse on my ongoing
perhaps with latent pique
that i smell of picnics
and you of routine

BETTER THINGS FOR BETTER LIVING
THROUGH PROVOCATION

There he goes,
a pest of a parvenu,
driving a convertible
whose price could keep a family going
for at least ten years.
For an alibi he displays
foreign, tax-exempt number plates.
See him swerving from lane to lane
at a speed not included on my speedometer,
and rendering every vehicle
the dunce cap of its driver.
And when a traffic light puts the kibosh on him,
watch him defenestrating sputum, curse and butt.
There he goes
whose style is in the huff,
exhaust transmitting a threatening broadcast
to a world lingering still in photostat.

We're in the doldrums, mates,
locked in our small geographies —
eavesdroppers on conversations with a Christ
who stoops to skim from the milk the cream.
But give us time, give us time,
and even snail-like we'll find a speed
to know each other truly by.

ROAD GANG

Haloed by humour that holds them buoyant
they go where a dream dies every day
in the still uncertain dawn
embroidering with their own blood
an endless pattern in their shirts.

Brotherthreaded through the eye of a needle
and caught in the act of themselves
they stoop to authenticate the irresolute times.
On their bull-like backs:
        hydrated melancholy of the fallow skies—
and still
                the earth demands of them
                        the precise analogy of sweat.

A blow of the pickax
            equals
                    Beethoven's *Pastorale*.
A flash of iron
            equals
                    the peacock crown of shahdom.
But the world goes by like a criminal
dumping a heavier affliction on their backs:
                        the affliction of scorn.

Variedly adjectival the common touch
but a common fortune can't be kept apart.
Fortitude shall endure
                    sublimely stratified
until they get old enough to be old in us
and live
        at last
                in our age.

CREW LIST, AS A FORM OF PRAYER

God bless
        the Master
                whose world is where the foot sinks
                and there is no miracle.
Bless
        the Mates and Engineers
                who lean on air in weight of weariness
                seeing that the sea has read them through.

God bless
        "Sparks"
                who looks for a voice
                in the flesh of silence.
Bless that character,
        the Purser,
                who's made more fathers
                than made him.
God bless
        "Chippy"
                who drunken
                thinks each sunset as a nipple
                and sober as a warp.
Bless
        the Bosun, the AB's, the Oilers and the Wipers
                who try to keep intact an image
                with its smell of femininity.
Bless
        the Stewards and the Cook
                who peel an incident
                from the newest absence.

And last but not least
        bless Dimitri from Orgáni
            aged sixteen
            rating: Deck Boy
                who must coarsen his nature
                to match his coarsened hands
        and live next to everything
        and close to nothing.

STREET SCENE

Like two warm stones together, laid dead true,
two blind men jab their tarnished tin cans into
the daily noise that has taken the place of the word.
A few look on with compassion,
but the fear of being thought old-fashioned
checks them a little, though perhaps not for the worse,
since the lips of one of the blind
find each other in a smile. And on they move,
examining prices like a doctor a patient's ills
and touching the purse with healing,
while the cheaply glistening stars
restore in opposition the downward impetus.

I stand
        without consistent stance
                    at the end of the queue
which makes pathless way
                            for what arrives.
On my brow rests the coolness
that comes down from the tree.
There is nothing gay
        or appealing
                    or proud in form,
everything takes shape
                            with obvious poorness.
I have the same wounded hand that men have,
the same foulmouthed silence,
the same doubt subsists in my scanty end,
and the same notion
        that this day perhaps
                    was never intended for me —
this day when people lose their jobs
in offices
        in factories
                    in the mines
and welfare is only a symptom of the times.

Athenians go to work.
A whole system of clocks
dies in their awaking.
They go
      on a coffee
           on a rusk
                on a newscast
            which adjusts them to ambivalence.
Athenians go to work
      thinking they're self-begotten
                at every place they pause.

They go,
dividing in two parts
everything they cross
      without ever learning
               or giving anything.
Athenians go to work
between faces that look and faces that see
between questions that answer and questions that knock —
they go with that delirious inability
      to come together
                like two pages.
What one of them talks about
the other one already knows.
Each goes no farther than
the other,
      or than himself.
Athenians go to work
pulled in two directions
and try to convince themselves
that they have the right of propriety:

And if they have to spend
        a moment of reason
                shaped like a smile
then I'm afraid
        a smile is
                    something else again.
Athenians pile up convictions
in their very depths
        that the slightest wind
                    can toss into the abyss.
Athenians start off at a greater speed than
their shadow
        with sterile defences
        with pitiful hopes
                    with a fist made of melancholy power —
they scurry through streets gaunt as a pencil
between houses with only veins of sky —
they go,
chewing up the way they stay alive
performing the faults they are fond of.
Athenians go to work,
go like needles of life looking for thread.
It is from those you meet
from those who still have a face
that one asks forgiveness
for those who no longer have any.

HOMEWARD THOUGHTS

Someone
in overalls
          is sitting on the fo'c'sle
        cupping his hands around
                    the live nothingness of life.
Another
is wearing dungarees
          blotched like a palette
        and scratches casually
                    his sexual trinity.
Five degrees to port
          and their hair-whipped faces
                    would be more finely assayed.
From the bridge:
          four bells in B-flat:
                    sound that conjugates
dark
      dark
            dark
                dark.

Mess-talk accompanies the engine's diphthongs.

Wind pleads upwards from the mast.

The man
in overalls
          adjusts himself on the bitt
        and expresses his doubts
                    on distant stars
which his mate repels
          still further
                    with his gaze.

Solitude extracts so much heart from the heart.

The stern caulks the prow's uncaulking;
and having to exist
            between
                  two potentates of yearning —
            between
                  the grimbrowed folding of the sea —
they fly softly from themselves
until they weep from such returning.

DESPITE BEING A POET

the firm's letterhead
gives my signature rank

in all the languages of men
only the rich will know my name

NOBLESSE OBLIGE

Men with money as their best technique
open dictionaries before obeying an impulse.
No simile
     no metaphor
         must sink roots into the heart.
No shadow must inch across the floor
beyond chronicled acceptance.
Take my uncle Nick:
     a masterpiece of taxidermy
         is his tight fist.
So mean is he
that there is a generation gap
between him and his clothes.

The discarded french letter
I count among his better turns.

THE STAINED-GLASS WINDOWS
OF METZ CATHEDRAL

Marc Chagall,
    whose gentile surplus was corrected
    by the blade at birth,
more than atoned for this excision
when he made a Christian fad of his art.
        Which makes me think
            that these pious parishioners
        are mere sycophants
    of his immaculate conception . . .

CORCOVADO

atop
his earth-
lit heaven,
as though stuck
half-way up
his ascension,
christ the redeemer
lends his weight
to material comfort,
powerless to affect
the intensity
of what becomes
oblivious

if this is blasphemy,
make most of it;
one needs such tenure
if one has no head
for heights . . .

Rio de Janeiro

COPACABANA

33

breakers paw impatiently
dare me to Atlantify my body
press on all the time
while the sun
    relaxes
        like a punctured tyre

a Bic-fingered youth
draws a huge heart on the sand
which he abandons
    to the sinews
        of wind

at least it has me to comfort it
where love doesn't exist

Rio de Janeiro

HARD TIMES

the poem flows from the pen
and drags its weary way
to the tenor yawning of an editor

refused, it works its darkness
into the gay winds that blow
about me in later spirit

WAITING FOR TANER BAYBARS,
Or Two Expectations Don't Make an Arrival

Midnight on the square,
and contrapuntal midnight
from a distant clock.
Then the quietness comes through
like a freak reception.

Chameleonic against a kiosk,
I wish that the moon would begin
at the beginning.
                    I wish —
(a blond youth comes in for a closer look;
I think he will not breach his discretion . . .)

Anyway,
the air now smells of people alighting
from a bus after a three-day journey,
and I must enter into the act of being
more than myself,
having already won doubt
from the now irrevocable youth.

COMING OF AGE

My elders have done with the diminutive.
Now they match me with themselves
and pour me brandy full of temperance.
And like a chair that has forgotten its tree
I must contain my own hardness.
With each new day cutting up lengths of yesterday
how much will the sun get to me?
I fear I will be left with a cheek in darkness,
the cheek one must always turn
that it may curdle into light.

True,
I humble no emotion to poetic precept,
preferring the crumpled paper on the desk.
It is also true
that I cannot face a whole day from dawn
for fear of outliving hope.
And look
it's taken me almost forty years
to even tell you my Christian name.
I know:
every bone is tied in a trance,
and I owe my life one jot of my soul.
But tell me, friend,
what do you do with an emptiness
that drives you back and forth in tides?

PUBLICATIONS

Take One! . . . Athens, APC, 1967.
Sorry, Wrong Number. London, Oasis Books, 1974.
V.H.F. Knotting, Bedfordshire, The Sceptre Press, 1974.
Athens Blues. London, Oasis Books, 1975.
Signing On. Knotting, Bedfordshire, The Sceptre Press, 1977.
Thorns in Each Other's Flesh. Hamilton, New Zealand, Outrigger Publishers, 1977.

Translator, *Aegeans and Other Poems* by Dimitris Christodoulou. Athens, Zarvanos, 1965.
Translator, *Nine Greek Poets.* Athens, APC, 1968.
Translator, *The Hydra of Birds,* Winchester, Hampshire, Green Horse Press, 1973.
Translator, *The Yellow House* by Alexandros Baras. London, Oasis Books, 1974.

Editor and translator, *Contemporary Greek Issue.* Mission, B.C., Canada, Contemporary Literature in Translation, 1977.

THE AUTHOR

YANNIS GOUMAS was born in Athens in 1940 into an old family of shipowners and seafarers from the islands of Spetsai and Andros on his father's side, and the island of Ithaki on his mother's side. When still very young he was taken to England, where he attended prep school, public school, and naval college. He served his cadetship on British vessels and as an officer on Greek ships which belonged to his family. After the ship on which he sailed sank in the Pacific, he joined a Greek shipping concern ashore, dividing his time between London and New York. During this period he collaborated with the BBC, the Central Office of Information, and various radio stations in the USA, as broadcaster and script-writer. In 1966 he gave up shipping and went to Greece. For the next four years he was engaged on research projects at the Athens Center of Ekistics (Doxiadis group). Simultaneously he had his own weekly show on television, recorded several songs which achieved popularity, was a disc jockey, acted on the stage, did advertising work, and conducted poetry readings. In 1974 he returned to the shipping community as vice-president and director in the family firm at Piraeus. His poetry has been translated into Turkish by Talât Sait Halman and Nermin Menemencioğlu, and into Serbo-Croat by Miodrag Pavlović.